About This Book

Title: *Kings and Queens*

Step: 3

Word Count: 149

Skills in Focus: Digraph ng

Tricky Words: people, queen, she, who, about, leads, leader, vote, lines

Ideas For Using This Book

Before Reading:

- **Comprehension:** Look at the title and cover image together. Ask: What do you know about kings and queens? Ask readers to make a prediction about what they might learn in the book.
- **Accuracy:** Practice saying the tricky words listed on page 1.
- **Phonics and Phonemic Awareness:** Tell students they will read words with the digraph *ng*. Explain that a digraph is two letters that make one sound. Write the word *ring* and have readers watch and listen as you segment the three sounds, pointing under each letter as you read. Be sure to point at the *n* and *g* together when you say the /ng/ sound! Ask the readers: What is the word? How many sounds are in the word? If students need help, tell them that *n* and *g* together make the sound /ng/. Repeat with *king* and *wing*.

During Reading:

- Have readers point under each word as they read it.
- **Decoding:** If readers are stuck on a word, help them say each sound and blend the sounds together smoothly. Be sure to point out words with *ng* as they appear.
- **Comprehension:** Invite readers to talk about new things they are learning about kings and queens while reading. What are they learning that they didn't know before?

After Reading:

Discuss the book. Some ideas for questions:
- What are kings and queens? What do they do?
- Have you read any stories with kings or queens? What happened in those stories?

Kings and Queens

Text by L. Bennett

Reading Consultant
Deborah MacPhee, PhD
Professor, School of Teaching and Learning
Illinois State University

PICTURE WINDOW BOOKS
a capstone imprint

4

What is a king? In the past, a king had a big job.

He was the boss.
He ran things.

People sang long songs at the top of their lungs about kings.

His dad was the king.

Then he got to be king.

What is a queen? In the past, she was the boss. She had lots of rings and bling.

Her dad was the king.

Then she got to be queen. She ran things.

Long ago, kings and queens ran things.

15

Now, we run things. A king or queen does not. We cast votes to pick who leads us.

He was a leader.
He ran things.

She was a leader.
She ran things.

But we have a job too.
We stand in long lines.
We pick who runs things!

If the leader did a good job running things, we cast a vote to say, Yes: Bring them back.

More Ideas:

Phonics and Phonemic Awareness Activity

Practicing Digraph *ng*:
Play I Spy! Prepare word cards with *ng* story words. Place each card face up on a surface. Choose a word to start the game. Say "I spy" and then segment the sounds in the word. For example, say "I spy /k/, /i/, /ng/." The readers will call out the word, then look for the corresponding card. Continue until all cards have been collected.

Suggested words:
• lungs
• long
• sang
• bring

Extended Learning Activity

Play Pretend:
Ask readers to pretend they are kings or queens for a day. Ask them what kind of place they would rule. Where would they live? What would they do there? Have readers draw a map of their kingdom.

George VI: 1; Henry VIII: 3, 9, 12; Charlemagne: 4;
Henry VII: 8; Victoria: 10–11; Elizabeth I: 13, 14–15

Published by Picture Window Books, an imprint of Capstone
1710 Roe Crest Drive, North Mankato, Minnesota 56003
capstonepub.com

Library of Congress Cataloging-in-Publication Data is available
on the Library of Congress website.

ISBN: 9798875227042 (hardback)
ISBN: 9798875229879 (paperback)
ISBN: 9798875229855 (eBook PDF)

Image Credits: iStock: clu, 18, duncan1890, cover, 8, 12, FierceAbin, 6–7,
Gwengoat, 9, 13, 24, LPETTET, 22–23, picture, 10–11, SDI Productions,
20–21, wynnter, 2–3, 14–15, ZU_09, 4–5; Shutterstock: Everett Collection,
16–17, Wally Stemberger, 1; Wikimedia Commons: Bain News Service/
Library of Congress Prints and Photographs Division, 19

Printed and bound in China. 6274